Québec

Québec

Janice Hamilton

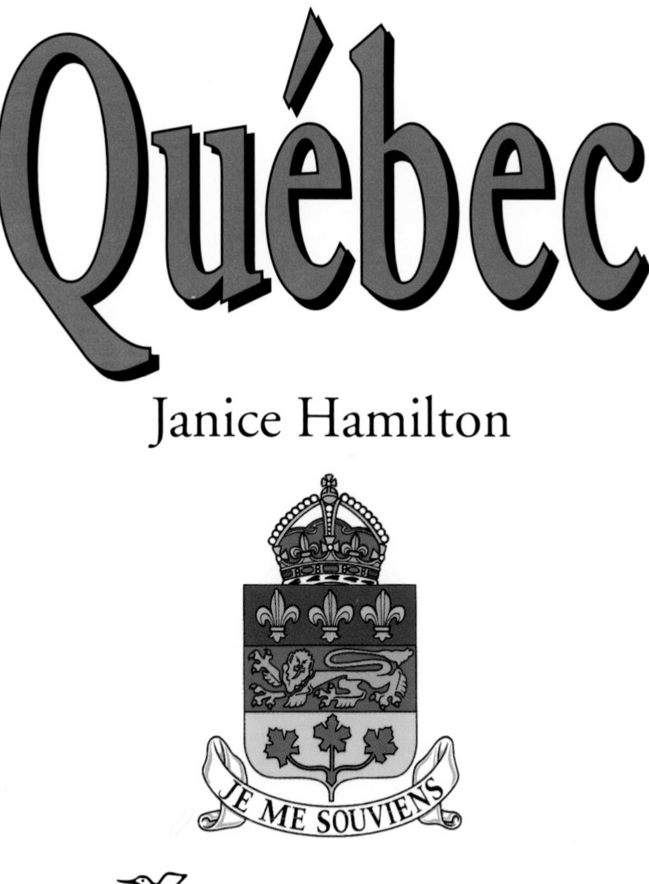

Fitzhenry & Whiteside

Lerner Web site address: www.lernerbooks.com

Published by Fitzhenry & Whiteside, 195 Allstate Parkway, Markham, Ontario under an arrangement with Lerner Publications Company, a division of Lerner Publishing Group.

Fitzhenry & Whiteside Web site address: www.fitzhenry.ca

National Library of Canada Cataloguing in Publication

Hamilton, Janice
Québec / Janice Hamilton. -- Rev. ed.
(Hello Canada)
Includes index.
ISBN 1-55041-764-9
1. Quebec (Province)--Juvenile literature. I. Title. II. Series.
FC2911.2.H25 2002 j971.4 C2002-903072-2
F1052.4.H36 2002

Fitzhenry & Whiteside acknowledges with thanks the Canada Council for the Arts, the Government of Canada through its Book Publishing Industry Development Program, and the Ontario Arts Council for their support in our publishing program.

Printed and bound in Hong Kong
2 3 4 5 6 7 – JR – 03 02 01 00 99 98

Cover photograph by Tony La Gruth. Background photo by R. Chen/SuperStock.

The glossary that starts on page 68 gives definitions of words shown in **bold type** in the text.

Senior Editor
Gretchen Bratvold
Editors
Lori Coleman
Domenica Di Piazza
Photo Researcher
Cindy Hartmon Nelson
Series Designer
Steve Foley

We would like to thank Montréal author and journalist Dominique Clift and Professor Brian Young of the History Department at McGill University for their help in preparing this book.

Contents

Fun Facts

Montréal, Québec, is the second largest French-speaking city in the world after Paris, France.

Samuel de Champlain, the explorer and founder of New France, died in what is now Québec City in 1635. Experts know where his grave site is but aren't sure the body inside is his.

Montmorency Falls near Québec City is Québec's highest waterfall. Plunging 76 metres (251 feet), the waterfall is almost 30 metres (100 feet) higher than Niagara Falls on the border between Ontario and New York.

Ice hockey was born in Québec. British soldiers who were stationed there in the early 1800s played the game with sticks and a ball. In 1875 a university student in Montréal substituted a round wooden puck for the ball and wrote down a set of rules.

The game Trivial Pursuit was invented in 1980 by a sports reporter and a newspaper photographer from Montréal. The two friends came up with the idea in half an hour, but they worked for many months to research and write all the questions.

Québec produces more maple syrup than any other province in Canada.

A pail fastened under a spout collects the sweet, gooey maple sap for making maple syrup and candy.

Signs near Quebec's border give information in both French and English.

Where the River Narrows

Québec, a province in eastern Canada, is like no place else in North America. Among the many differences people notice are highway and advertising signs written in French. This is because most of the people who live in Québec speak French, the province's official language. Three times the size of France, Québec has the largest land area of the 10 Canadian provinces. And Québec is the second largest province in population.

Québec is one of the biggest and most populated regions in Canada.

Québec's name comes from the Algonquian Indian word *kebec,* which means "the place where the river narrows." French explorer Samuel de Champlain gave this name to the settlement he founded in 1608 at what is now Québec City, on the shores of the St. Lawrence River. The word also was eventually applied to the entire province. The St. Lawrence River flows northeast from Lake Ontario—one of the five **Great Lakes**—to the broad Gulf of St. Lawrence. West of Québec City, the wide river becomes narrow.

On a map, Québec resembles the shape of a triangle. To the west lie the province of Ontario and the cold waters of James and Hudson Bays. Along Québec's southern border are the U.S. states of New York, Vermont, New

A lighthouse (right) ***in Forillon National Park overlooks the Gulf of St. Lawrence. The St. Lawrence River*** (facing page) ***flows past Québec City toward the Gulf of St. Lawrence. As the river approaches the gulf, the water becomes increasingly salty, making it a good home for beluga whales*** (lower right). ***But pollution in the river has killed many belugas, lowering their population from many thousands to about 500.***

Hampshire, and Maine, as well as the Canadian province of New Brunswick. The waves of the Gulf of St. Lawrence, an arm of the Atlantic Ocean, lap against Québec's southeastern shores. The province of Newfoundland and Labrador borders Québec to the east. Across Ungava Bay and Hudson Strait to the north is the new territory of Nunavut.

The drawing of Québec on the facing page is called a physical map. It shows physical features such as coasts, islands, mountains, rivers and lakes. The colours represent a range of elevations, or heights above sea level (see legend box). This map also outlines each of Québec's geographical regions. The map on this page, called a political map, mainly locates features created by people, including cities, roads, railways and parks.

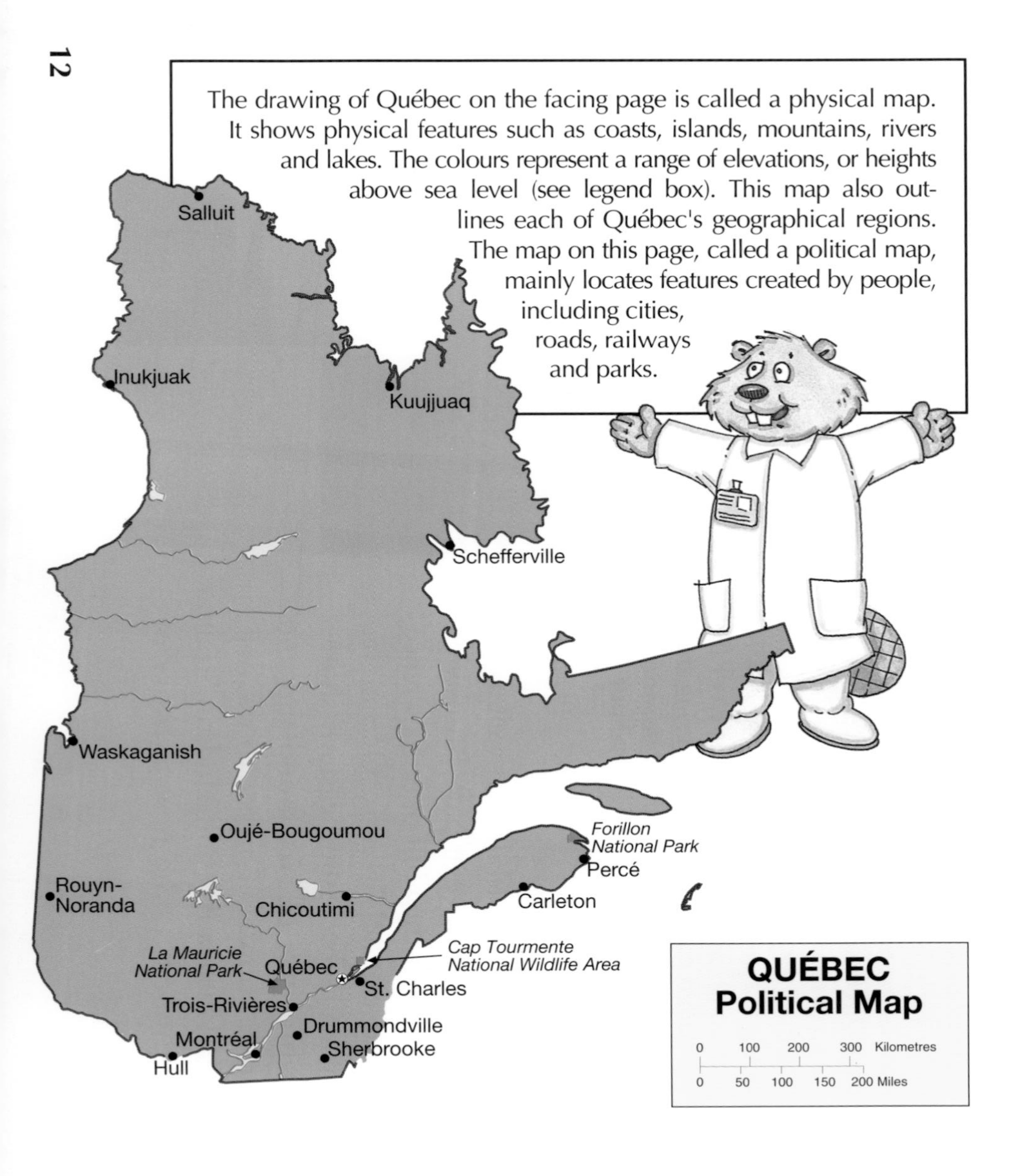

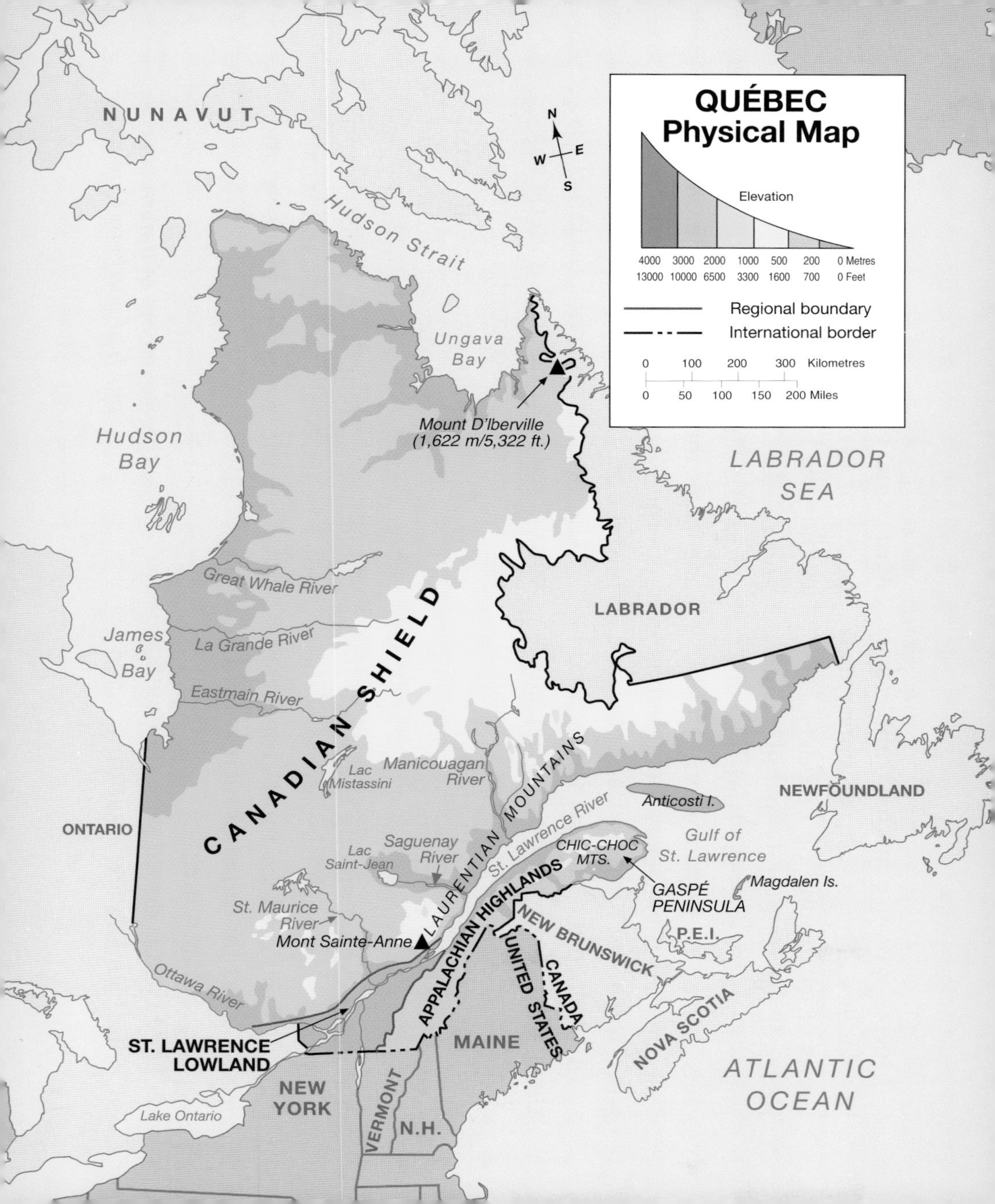
QUÉBEC
Physical Map
Elevation
4000 3000 2000 1000 500 200 0 Metres
13000 10000 6500 3300 1600 700 0 Feet
Regional boundary
International border
0 100 200 300 Kilometres
0 50 100 150 200 Miles
N
W
E
S
NUNAVUT
Hudson Strait
Ungava Bay
Mount D'Iberville
(1,622 m/5,322 ft.)
Hudson Bay
LABRADOR SEA
LABRADOR
Great Whale River
James Bay
La Grande River
Eastmain River
CANADIAN SHIELD
Lac Mistassini
Manicouagan River
LAURENTIAN MOUNTAINS
ONTARIO
Anticosti I.
NEWFOUNDLAND
Lac Saint-Jean
Saguenay River
St. Lawrence River
CHIC-CHOC MTS.
Gulf of St. Lawrence
GASPÉ PENINSULA
Magdalen Is.
St. Maurice River
Mont Sainte-Anne
APPALACHIAN HIGHLANDS
NEW BRUNSWICK
UNITED STATES
CANADA
P.E.I.
NOVA SCOTIA
Ottawa River
ST. LAWRENCE LOWLAND
MAINE
ATLANTIC OCEAN
NEW YORK
VERMONT
N.H.
Lake Ontario

Québec was once covered completely by **glaciers**. These vast, slow-moving sheets of ice ground up boulders, carried soil for thousands of miles, and gouged out holes in the land. The glaciers started to retreat about 15,000 years ago. As the glaciers melted, they filled the holes, forming lakes.

In Québec the glaciers left behind three main land regions—the Canadian Shield, the St. Lawrence Lowland, and the Appalachian Highlands. The Canadian Shield covers the northern 80 percent of the province. Some of the Shield's rocks are among the oldest in the world. Although the climate of the Shield is too cold for most crops, the region is rich in minerals such as gold, copper, and iron ore.

The Shield is dotted with thousands of ponds and lakes, including Lake Mistassini, the province's largest lake. Some of Québec's biggest rivers, including the Eastmain, the Great Whale, and the La Grande Rivers, flow west across the Shield into James Bay. The Saguenay, the St. Maurice, the Ottawa, and the Manicouagan Rivers empty into the St. Lawrence River to the east.

The northern part of the Shield is considered **tundra**. In this arctic area, the climate is too cold for trees to grow. Only plants such as lichens, mosses, and low-growing shrubs can survive. Animals on the tundra include foxes, arctic hare, caribou, and polar bears. Seals, walrus, and whales swim in the waters of Hudson and Ungava Bays.

Large stretches of tundra cover much of northern Québec.

Mont Sainte-Anne (left) ***is a popular spot for skiing in the Laurentian Mountains. White-water rafters*** (inset) ***enjoy the region's briskly flowing rivers. Wolverines*** (above) ***live throughout the Canadian Shield, hunting rodents and larger animals for food.***

South of the tundra, in the warmer part of the Canadian Shield, forests of spruce, fir, and tamarack trees grow. Moose, deer, black bears, and raccoon make their homes in these wooded areas.

Along the southeastern edge of the Canadian Shield rises a mountain range called the Laurentian Mountains, or Laurentides. Formed billions of years ago, the range has been worn down by wind and water but still contains some of the province's highest peaks. Many people spend weekends at inns and cottages in the Laurentides, where they can ski and hike.

Most of the cities in the Shield region are small. Many concentrate around the mining and timber industries. The main towns include Chicoutimi and Rouyn-Noranda. The city of Hull is a centre for Canadian government offices. Farmers near Lac Saint-Jean raise dairy cattle, potatoes, and blueberries.

The St. Lawrence Lowland region spreads along both sides of the upper St. Lawrence River. The waterway is one of the most important routes to the interior of the North American continent. Many freshwater fish swim in the river. Sea mammals such as seals and whales can also be seen.

Nine out of ten Quebecers live in the St. Lawrence Lowland. Farmers there grow crops in the fertile soil and raise dairy cattle. The province's two largest cities—Montréal and Québec City, the capital—are in the lowland.

The remains of eight ancient volcanoes called the Monteregian Hills rise in the southwestern part of the St.

Farms sprawl across large portions of the St. Lawrence Lowland.

Lawrence Lowland. The best-known hill is Mount Royal, located in the heart of Montréal. Homes, offices, and the campuses of McGill University and the Université de Montréal creep up Mount Royal's lower slopes. At the top is a park where Montrealers cross-country ski in winter and picnic in summer.

Montréal, with a population of about three million, is Canada's second largest city, after Toronto in Ontario. Montréal is built on an island near where the Ottawa and St. Lawrence Rivers meet.

The Chic-Choc Mountains, part of the Appalachian Highlands, feature a barren, rocky landscape.

The peaks and hills of the Appalachian Highlands are part of the Appalachian Mountains—a chain that stretches from eastern Canada to the U.S. state of Alabama. The Appalachian region in Québec includes the Gaspé Peninsula, a forested tongue of land that juts out into the Gulf of St. Lawrence. The Eastern Townships, a farming and tourism area southeast of Montréal, is also part of the Appalachian Highlands. Sherbrooke is the largest city in the region.

Québec has a climate that varies from north to south. In northern areas, summers are cool and winters are long and bitterly cold. In southern cities such as Montréal, summers can be very hot and humid, while winters are usually cold and snowy. The average July temperature in Montréal is 26° C (78° F), while northern areas may average only 7° C (45° F). In January, Montréalers expect temperatures around –6° C (21° F). Residents in northern towns such as Schefferville often see their thermometers drop to –30° C (–21° F).

Northern Québec receives less **precipitation** (rain and snow) than the southern part of the province. When it snows in the north, for example, residents can count on an average of at least 175 centimetres (69 inches). People in Montréal, on the other hand, may have to shovel about 234 centimetres (92 inches) of snow each year.

For the Birds

Gannets

Common loon

Snowy owl

Québec is home to about 350 species of birds each summer. For example, 25,000 pairs of white seabirds called gannets nest on Bonaventure Island. Each spring and fall, huge flocks of snow geese stop to rest near Québec City on their way to and from their nesting sites farther north. But only sparrows, snowy owls, and a few other hardy birds remain in the province all year.

The Early Years

Aboriginal peoples first settled in the St. Lawrence River Valley about 6,000 years ago. By the 1500s, many different groups of people were living in what is now the province of Québec. Among them were several groups of Algonquian speakers, including the Algonquin, Abenaki, and Mi'kmaq. They survived in the eastern woodlands of Québec mainly by fishing, by gathering roots and berries, and by hunting game.

These Aboriginals lived in dome-shaped dwellings made from tree branches and covered with bark or animal skins. In summer people travelled by water in birchbark canoes. In winter they crossed the deep snow on snowshoes. Clothes made from animal furs kept people warm.

The Abenaki built canoes from birchbark and decorated their sides with etchings. Abenaki snowshoes were constructed with pieces of wood and strips of leather.

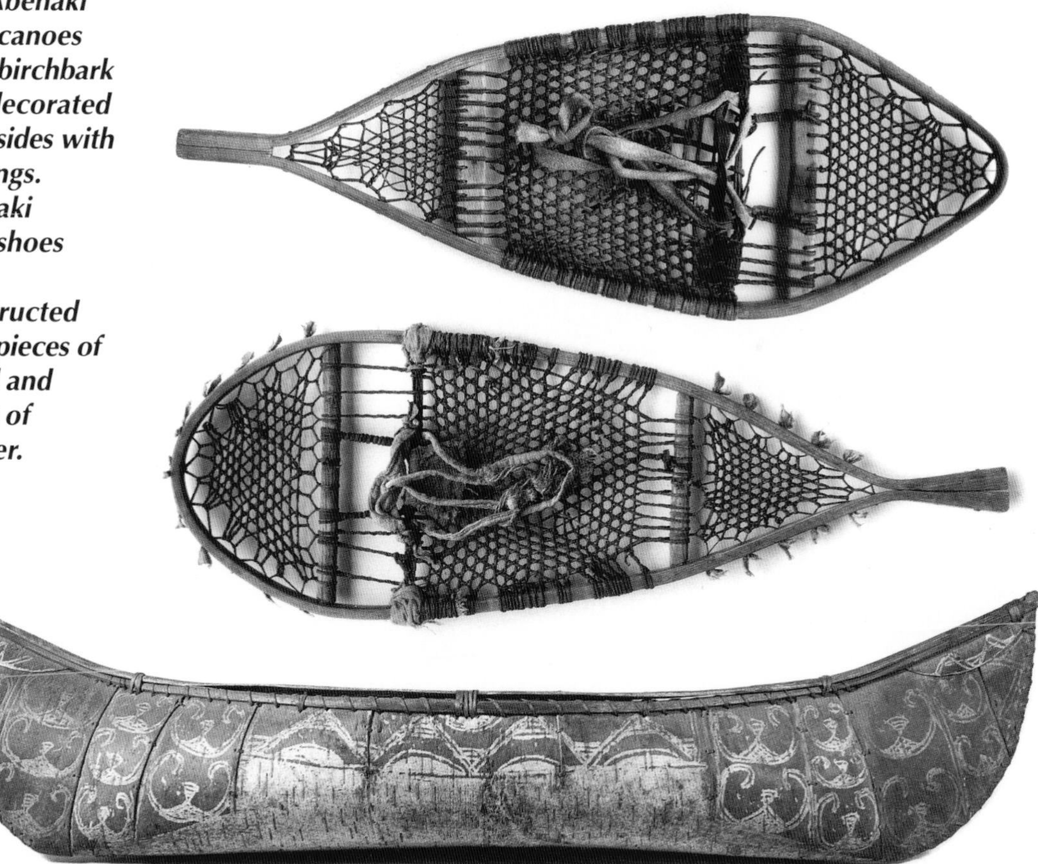

Two other Algonquian groups, the Cree and the Innu, lived in northern Québec. These Aboriginal peoples moved throughout their territories hunting geese and tracking moose and caribou. Families relied on the animals' meat for food and used the hides and antlers to make clothing and tools.

Using traditional methods, the Cree people of Waskaganish in northern Québec stretch out beaver skins to dry in the sun.

The territories of the Huron and the Iroquois people, who spoke Iroquoian, extended from what is now New York and Ontario into the lowlands of the St. Lawrence River. These groups cleared forestland to plant crops such as corn, beans, and squash. They also hunted deer, beavers, and bears for food and for materials to make clothing. Families lived in small villages of bark-covered dwellings called longhouses.

Inuit people lived along the shores of Hudson and Ungava Bays in Québec's far north. The Inuit fished, and they also hunted whales, seals, and other sea mammals. For water transportation, they crafted long, narrow boats called kayaks. Families lived in winter homes built from blocks of snow. During warmer months, they constructed tents from driftwood and caribou hides.

An early French drawing portrays an Inuit hunter with his hunting gear and kayak paddle.

In 1534 French explorer Jacques Cartier nosed his ship into the Gulf of St. Lawrence. He was looking for gold and for a water route to Asia. Cartier put up a cross on the Gaspé coast to claim the land for the king of France and then sailed home.

The next summer, Cartier returned and explored the St. Lawrence River as far south as the Huron village of Hochelaga (present-day Montréal). Cartier and his crew built a small fort near Stadacona (another Huron village near what is now Québec City). But the Europeans were not prepared for cold weather. In addition, almost everyone became sick with a disease called scurvy. Local Aboriginals offered a cure—cedar bark tea.

Jacques Cartier, known for his explorations of the St. Lawrence River Valley, made three separate trips to the area from his native France.

Curious about Iroquois stories of gold and other treasures, Cartier returned to what is now Québec in 1541. He collected what he thought were gold and diamonds, but they turned out to be worthless stones.

After that disappointment, the only Europeans interested in the region were fur traders. Felt hats made from beaver pelts were very popular in France. Aboriginals in Québec trapped beavers and traded the furs to Europeans in return for kettles, cloth, and liquor.

In 1608 French explorer Samuel de Champlain built the Habitation du Québec—a fort and a warehouse on the St. Lawrence River. The small settlement was the first permanent French colony in North America, and Champlain became known as the Father of New France.

French traders travelled from one Aboriginal village to the next, hoping to exchange blankets, knives, guns, and tools for furs and pemmican—a mixture of dried meat, dried berries, and fat.

Some of the early settlers in New France were labourers, craftspeople, fishers, and farmers. But most European residents of the small colony were either fur traders or Roman Catholic **missionaries**, who came to teach their religion to Aboriginals. Over time, many Aboriginals became sick from European diseases such as measles, influenza, and smallpox. Because the Aborigials had never been exposed to these illnesses, thousands of them died.

By the 1660s, New France had only about 3,000 settlers. The king of France realized that for the colony to survive, it needed more settlers.

About 2,600 French newcomers arrived in the colony between 1665 and 1672. Some of the men were farmers. Others were soldiers sent to protect French settlers from attacks by the Iroquois, who were trying to maintain control of their fur-rich lands in New France. Ships also brought young women—many of them orphans—looking for marriage and a new life. The French government offered rewards to couples who had large families, and the population of New France grew quickly.

Meanwhile, British merchants were also interested in the fur trade in North America. They sent a ship to explore Hudson Bay, returning home with a boatload of rich furs. In 1670 the British king granted a fur-trading outfit called the Hudson's Bay Company control of all land with rivers flowing into Hudson Bay. This territory, known as Rupert's Land, included all of what is now northern Québec.

The British and the French fought many battles for control of North America and the fur trade. In 1759, during the Seven Years' War (1756–1763), British troops approached Québec City. The soldiers tried to attack several times, but the town was too well defended. Finally, the British troops landed upriver, climbed the cliff during the night, and surprised the French on a farmer's field known as the Plains of Abraham. The British won the battle after only 15 minutes. A year later, Montréal was attacked and New France surrendered. After the war ended in 1763, the French colony became part of British North America and was called the Province of Quebec.

Life in New France

New France had three main towns in what is now the province of Québec—Montréal, Trois-Rivières, and Québec. Québec was the capital of the colony, and the governor and other government officials made their homes in the town. Québec also had a busy port, where workers unloaded supplies from France or loaded boats with furs to send overseas.

Trois-Rivières and Montréal were both important fur-trade centres. The highlight of the year was Montréal's fur market in June. For this bustling event, Aboriginals came to town to trade beaver pelts for European goods such as blankets and hatchets.

Most people in New France lived in the country, far away from towns. The government of New France gave out long, narrow parcels of land, called seigneuries, to the colony's wealthy merchants, army officers, and government officials. The seigneurs, or landlords, rented the land to farmers called habitants. Farmhouses were usually built of wood and heated with a large fireplace.

In the countryside, habitants cleared trees from the land and grew crops such as corn, cabbage, wheat, and oats to feed their families. The farmers also raised cows, sheep, pigs, oxen, and horses. Women mostly worked in the home, cooking meat pies, baking bread, and smoking fish. Smoked eel was a favourite dish

Nowadays, if you fly over Québec's farmland, you can see that much of the land is still divided into the long, narrow shape of the seigneuries. Although the colonists of New France are long gone, their way of shaping the land is still part of modern life.

Many differences separated the new English-speaking rulers and their French-speaking subjects. While most British were Protestants, the French Canadians were Roman Catholics. Each group also followed a different system of laws. To gain the support of their new subjects, the British passed the Québec Act in 1774. This law ensured that French citizens could continue to practise their laws and religion.

With the end of the American Revolution in 1783, Great Britain lost control of its colonies to the United

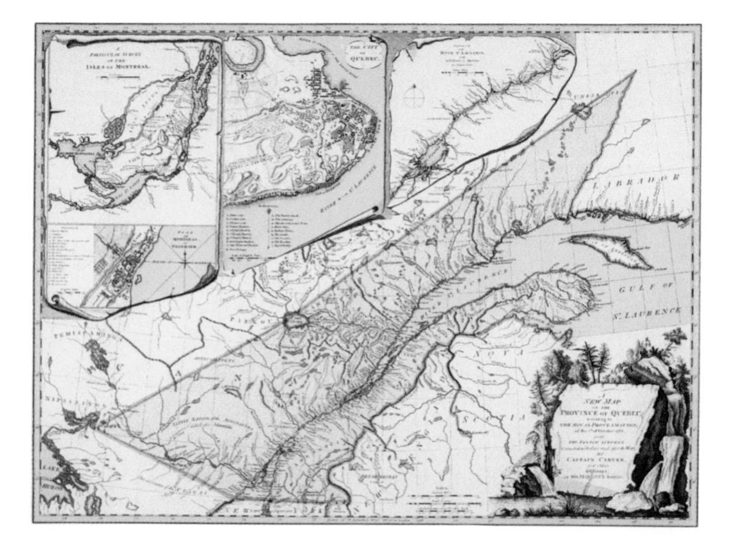

A map (left) ***of the Province of Quebec shows how the area—including Montréal and Québec City—had grown by 1763. In 1792, after the province was divided in two, parliament members of Lower Canada*** (facing page) ***met in Québec to discuss the new political unit.***

States. **Loyalists,** or colonists who had supported the British during the Revolution, flooded into Québec.

Some Loyalists settled in the Eastern Townships and in Montréal, but most moved west. The Loyalists, however, didn't like living under French laws. So in 1791, the British government divided the province in two—Upper Canada and Lower Canada. Most French speakers lived in Lower Canada, along the St. Lawrence River. English speakers resided mainly in Upper Canada, which is now Ontario. Each section kept its own laws and language.

Upper Canada and Lower Canada were each run by a governor chosen by Great Britain. Each governor picked a council of advisers—many of them wealthy merchants, landowners, and church leaders. Although local voters elected representatives to an assembly, the group did not have any real power over the governor or the council.

Times of Growth and Change

The beginning of the 1800s brought great hardship to the people of Lower Canada. Bad weather and plant diseases caused many crops to fail. A large number of farm families had barely enough food to survive.

In addition waves of immigrants from England, Ireland, and Scotland began arriving at the port of Québec City after 1815. Many were penniless and some carried deadly diseases that spread and killed thousands of Lower Canadians.

Most of the newcomers moved on to Upper Canada. But enough stayed in Lower Canada that by 1831 Montréal and Québec City were home to large numbers of British people. Some French Canadians worried that their language and culture would be lost.

A group of French Canadian leaders wanted to protect the French language and traditions of Lower Canada. In 1826 they formed a political party called the Parti Patriote. The Patriotes demanded that French Canadians have more say in running their affairs. The British rejected the idea and conflict broke out during the Rebellion of 1837. Facing well-armed British soldiers, the ill-prepared French Canadian Patriotes were quickly defeated.

The British army overcame the Patriote soldiers in St. Charles, Québec, in 1837.

Britain sent the Earl of Durham to Canada to find out what had caused the rebellion. Lord Durham wrote a report that claimed the problems in Canada would disappear if the French adopted British ways. He thought this would happen if Lower and Upper Canada were joined. So in 1841, Britain united Lower and Upper Canada as the Province of Canada. Lower Canada became Canada East, and Upper Canada was known as Canada West. English became the official language of the new province.

Meanwhile, Canada East's economy was growing. Lumberjacks chopped down trees and floated the logs on the St. Lawrence River to Québec City, where the timber was loaded onto ships bound for Britain. Canals were built in the 1840s, improving transportation around rapids on the St. Lawrence River. Workers laid railroad tracks, linking Montréal with Canada West and the United States.

With better transportation, Montréal was easier to reach, and industries grew. Many people moved to the city, where they found jobs in beer breweries, flour mills, and sugar refineries. Labourers were hired to build railway equipment and steamboats. Many of these industries were owned by Montrealers of English and Scottish origin.

In the mid-1800s, Canadian leaders began to talk about uniting the British colonies in North America. Together, the colonies would be more powerful. Many French Canadians liked the idea. They thought that by forming a province within a larger country, the French could control their own affairs.

By the 1840s, railroads linked many towns in Canada East.

Québec City in the mid-1800s was a thriving port and commercial centre.

In 1867 the British government divided the Province of Canada into two separate provinces—Ontario and Québec. Together with Nova Scotia and New Brunswick, the provinces formed a new country—the Dominion of Canada.

Despite Montréal's thriving businesses, most people in Québec lived on small farms in the country. By 1880 thousands of French Canadians had moved to the United States to look for better paying work. To encourage people to stay in Québec, the government gave French Canadians farmland in the Lac Saint-Jean region, in Gaspé, and in the Laurentides.

In 1898 a dam was built at Shawinigan—a waterfall on the St. Maurice River, north of Trois-Rivières. The water held back by the dam was slowly released to turn engines that produced **hydroelectricity.** With this affordable form of energy, pulp and paper mills and other industries sprung up near the town.

Gold and copper mines eventually opened in northwestern Québec as well. By the early 1900s, pulp and paper mills along the Ottawa, St. Maurice, and Saguenay Rivers turned Québec into the world's leading producer of newsprint for newspapers.

During the 1930s, a worldwide economic depression left many people without jobs. In Montréal 40 percent of working people lost their jobs. Even more workers were unemployed in remote communities such as Chicoutimi, where pulp and paper plants—the main employers in the area—closed.

Canada's economy improved during World War II (1939–1945). Workers in Québec refined aluminum to build airplanes and other wartime equipment. Textile and chemical manufacturing as well as the production of powdered milk and other food items in Québec boomed during the war. After the war, workers in the province built new schools, roads, and dams.

Maurice Duplessis was the premier, or provincial leader, of Québec from 1936 to 1939 and again from 1944 to 1959. Many people accused the powerful leader of slowing progress in Québec, but Duplessis had the support of church and business leaders.

In 1960 voters in Québec elected the Liberal Party into power. The government then made changes that swept every corner of Québec's society and politics. This period of reform (1960–1966) became known as the Quiet Revolution.

Among many kinds of changes, Québec's French-speaking majority began to refer to themselves by a French word—Québécois—rather than as French Canadians. Québec's government took control of the province's schools and hospitals from the Catholic Church. The provincial government also took charge of all private power companies and set up a government-owned power company called Hydro-Québec. In 1968 Hydro-Québec opened the biggest dam in the world on the Manicouagan River in northeastern Québec.

For many years, some of Québec's citizens have wondered whether Québec would be better off as a nation separate from Canada. Support for independence increased during the Quiet Revolution.

In 1976 voters in Québec elected into power the Parti Québécois (PQ), a political party that favours in-

A Question of Language **—** For many years, Francophones (French speakers) and Anglophones (English speakers) in Québec and throughout Canada have struggled over which of the two languages should be used in schools, in businesses, and in courts and other government bodies. Finally in 1969, Canada passed a law called the Official Languages Act, making both French and English the country's official national languages.

In Québec, where more than 80 percent of the population speak French, lawmakers passed Bill 101 in 1977, making French the province's official language. As a result, French is taught in schools, spoken in the workplace, and used in courts and other government offices all over the province.

dependence. PQ founder René Lévesque became the province's premier. In 1980 Québec held a **referendum** (special vote) on whether to separate from Canada. Sixty percent of voters rejected the idea.

Following the referendum, the governments of Canada and Québec tried to decide on new powers for Québec within Canada. Each time they failed to come to an agreement. In 1994 voters in Québec elected a new PQ government. The government held another referendum on Québec independence in October 1995. By barely a percentage point (50.6 to 49.4) Quebecers said "No" to building a smaller, separate nation. "Yes" leaders, including Lucien Bouchard, Québec's premier, vowed they would continue to work toward another vote on the issue. In the meantime, Quebecers will continue to plan for their future as citizens of Canada.

A welder in Trois-Rivières works on a part for a paper-making machine. Manufacturing employs almost one-fifth of all Québec's workers.

On the Job in Québec

In 1922, 15-year-old Joseph-Armand Bombardier from the village of Valcourt, Québec, designed a motorized vehicle to travel over snow. Today's version of Bombardier's invention is the snowmobile! Based in Montréal, Bombardier, Inc., now manufactures and sells all kinds of transportation equipment, including railcars and airplanes.

Manufacturing jobs employ 17 percent of Québec's workforce. Most large factories in Québec are located around Montréal. More than 60,000 workers at food-processing plants make pastas, butter, cheeses, soups, beers, soft drinks, and other manufactured products. Some of the clothes Canadians wear are sewn in Montréal as well.

More than half of Québec is forested. Thousands of workers in the province fashion Québec's logs into door frames, furniture, lumber, and other wood products. The province turns out 7 million metric tons (7.7 million tons) of pulp and paper each year, about one-third of all the pulp and paper produced in Canada. Workers also manufacture paper bags, boxes, and toilet paper. Newsprint for newspapers is one of Québec's most important exports, or goods traded to other nations.

An ocean freighter awaits its cargo of lumber at Carleton, a port in southeastern Québec.

When logging companies cut down trees, they are required to replant the area to make sure enough trees remain for future generations. Millions of new trees have been planted in Québec's forests since this law was passed in 1978.

Many workers in Québec have jobs with companies that make cellular telephones and other telecommunications equipment. Other workers manufacture cars, buses, aircraft, satellites, chemicals, metal tools, machinery, and aluminum sheeting.

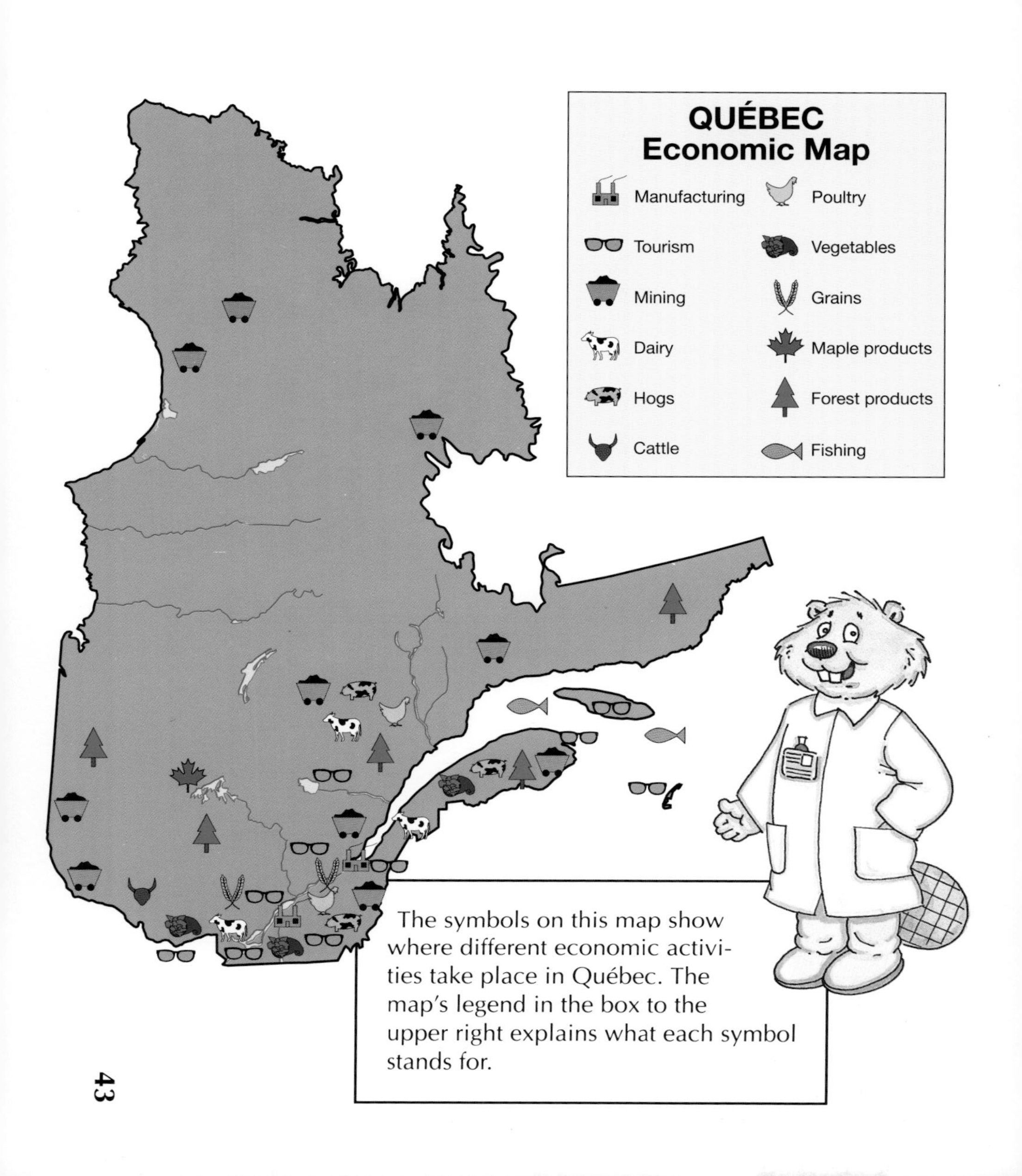

The symbols on this map show where different economic activities take place in Québec. The map's legend in the box to the upper right explains what each symbol stands for.

The James Bay and Northern Québec Agreement

In 1971 the government of Québec announced a plan for Hydro-Québec to build a giant power project in northern Québec. To create more hydroelectricity for homes and businesses, the company wanted to dam several rivers that flow into James Bay. But the Cree and the Inuit who live in the region said they didn't want the dams or the power plants on their ancestral lands. They took the government to court to prevent construction.

After four years of negotiation, the Aboriginals signed the James Bay and Northern Québec Agreement. The agreement allowed Hydro-Québec to begin work on the first stage of construction. In return, the Cree and the Inuit preserved their right to hunt, fish, and trap on the land. In addition, they received money to run their own schools, health clinics, and government affairs.

Ten years later, Hydro-Québec completed the first stage of the power project. Workers re-routed five rivers and built three powerhouses. They also built huge reservoirs, or lakes, behind the dams to store water for powering the engines that create electricity.

But these reservoirs have flooded the land, destroying traditional hunting areas used by Aboriginals. And the water in the reservoirs dissolved mercury, a poisonous chemical found naturally in plants and soil. As a result, mercury contaminated fish that Inuit and Cree families traditionally depended on for food. Now many Aboriginals have to buy expensive canned and packaged foods instead of eating freshly caught fish.

When the provincial government was ready to build additional dams in the north, Aboriginal leaders and environmentalists fought hard against the idea. They wanted to protect the land and the Aboriginals' way of life. Their work paid off, and the government put the project on hold in 1994.

Hydroelectric dams on Québec's rivers provide most of the electricity needed to run machinery and equipment in the province's factories. Hydro-Québec is one of the province's largest companies and is the largest producer of electricity in Canada. Unlike power produced from burning coal, hydroelectric power does not create air pollution.

Students and their teacher study nature at the Cap Tourmente National Wildlife Area near Québec City.

Some of the many tourists who come to Québec each year visit Québec's giant hydroelectric stations. The province also draws tourists with its concerts, museums, and recreational activities. Tourism provides service jobs for many Quebecers. Instead of manufacturing a product, service workers help people and businesses. About 75 percent of Québec's labour force has service jobs. These workers include doctors, nurses, teachers, lawyers, cooks, waiters, and salespeople.

Many service workers have jobs in office towers in downtown Montréal, where the headquarters of major banks, insurance companies, and real estate agencies are located. Other service workers have jobs with the provincial government in Québec City.

Because few roads reach remote areas of northern Québec, many people who live there rely on snowmobiles for winter transportation.

Montréal's underground subway system carries commuters and sightseers all around town.

Thousands of service workers in Québec have transportation jobs, helping people and goods reach their destinations. The Montréal area, for example, is a crossroads of water, rail, highway, and air traffic. Although Montréal lies 1,609 kilometres (1,000 miles) from the Atlantic Ocean, the city has one of the biggest ports in Canada. The canals and dams of the St. Lawrence Seaway, completed in 1959, allow large freight-carrying ships to bypass the river's rapids and travel easily between the Great Lakes and the Atlantic Ocean.

The Canadian Coast Guard operates ships with specially strengthened hulls that break through ice on the St. Lawrence, keeping the Montréal port open for ships year-round. The Canadian National Railway is headquartered in Montréal, and the city also boasts two international airports.

Québec has a rich supply of mineral resources, but less than 1 percent of the province's workers have mining jobs. A giant iron ore mine near the Labrador border was closed in the 1980s because of a decrease in demand. Some miners in Québec unearth copper and zinc. Others scoop up limestone, sand, and gravel for making roads. A large new nickel mine is being developed in Québec's far north.

Gold flecks shine in a piece of rock mined in Québec. Most of Québec's gold is mined in the southwestern corner of the province.

About 2 percent of Québec's workers have jobs in agriculture. Farmers in Québec raise pigs, beef cattle, and chickens. They grow corn, apples, and vegetables such as carrots and potatoes. Québec has the largest dairy industry in Canada. Most dairy cattle, as well as crops, are raised in the fertile St. Lawrence Lowland region.

Québec's farms (left) ***produce grains and vegetables, some of which are sold at open-air markets*** (above) ***in Montréal and in Québec City.***

Cree fishers (right) ***pull freshwater fish from under the thick ice in winter. After returning from a fishing trip, workers at Percé*** (above) ***clean their catches on shore.***

Some commercial fishers haul in crabs from the lower St. Lawrence River. For many years, fishers cruised the Gulf of St. Lawrence off the Gaspé Peninsula for cod. But overfishing of cod threatened to wipe out the fish, so in the early 1990s, cod fishing was banned along Canada's eastern coast. For this reason, more people are out of work in the Gaspé region than anywhere else in the province. But overall, with its mighty rivers, vast forests, and skilled workers, Québec faces the 21st century with a solid economy.

An Island in the Sea

Every June 24, Quebecers celebrate a provincial holiday called Saint-Jean-Baptiste Day. A big parade in Montréal is followed by a televised outdoor concert and fireworks. Towns and neighbourhoods across the province organize picnics and other festivities. Many people hang Québec's flag from their balconies. Children paint blue-and-white *fleurs de lys* (lilies, the provincial flower) on their faces. This is the day residents celebrate their pride in being from Québec.

Children (opposite page) ***carry small Québec flags that feature the fleur de lys, the provincial symbol. A lively parade*** (above) ***honouring Saint-Jean-Baptiste highlights Québec's big provincial celebration each June. Many festivals in Québec are topped off with a colourful display of fireworks*** (inset).

Québec's population is nearly 7 million. Almost 6 million Quebecers are Francophones, whose native language is French. Many are descendants of the original settlers who came from France during the 1600s. Francophones learn English at school, and many speak both languages easily.

Most English-speaking Quebecers live in Montréal or in the Eastern Townships, where they go to English schools and hospitals. These people usually watch television, read, and attend plays and other cultural events in English. Many also speak French, which they learn at school.

One way the Québécois, or French Quebecers, maintain their culture is through Québec's four French-language television networks. Viewers in Québec can also choose between two English-language Canadian television networks and several U.S. stations.

A moviemaking crew goes to work on a documentary film centred in downtown Montréal.

The province prints newspapers in French and English. Montréal, for example, has one English-language paper and three French-language daily newspapers. Other cities in Québec, including the capital, also have daily French newspapers.

Quebecers are of many origins, including French (75 percent), British (4 percent), Italian (3 percent), and German, Greek, Polish, and Portuguese (less than 1 percent each). Aboriginal peoples make up about 1 percent of Québec's population. They include First Nations people, Inuit, and Métis—people of mixed Native Indian and European descent.

A saxophone player (above) ***and a trumpet player*** (right) ***entertain passersby in Montréal.***

The largest Aboriginal groups in the province include the Cree, the Mohawk, the Huron, the Innu, and the Inuit. Most Inuit families live along the coasts of Hudson and Ungava Bays in northern Québec. Some Aboriginal peoples live in small communities or on **reserves** (land set aside for Aboriginal nations by the government), some of which are close to big cities. Like their ancestors, many Aboriginal families spend part of the year hunting and fishing on the land, away from settlements.

Using traditional methods, Cree women in the village of Oujé-Bougoumou in northern Québec sew strips of rabbit fur to make a soft and warm bedspread.

Québec welcomes immigrants from all over the world. Recent immigrants have come from Vietnam and Haiti as well as from South American and Middle Eastern countries. Most newcomers settle in Montréal. Ethnic festivals, such as the Autumn Moon Festival in Chinatown and a midsummer parade hosted by the West Indian community, attract many people.

Québec's busy creative community includes hundreds of artists and writers. The Montréal Museum of Fine Arts is one of the oldest museums in Canada. Clothing, artifacts, and films at the Native Museum of Pointe-Bleue help teach viewers about Innu culture and history. At the Wendake Indian Reserve near Québec City, visitors watch Huron artists making snowshoes and other traditional items.

An artist in Québec carves a statue from a tree trunk.

In music, there's something for everyone, from pop concerts to the Montréal Symphony Orchestra. Dozens of theatre groups and dance companies entertain audiences. A circus school in Montréal trains performers aged 12 and older in juggling and other circus skills. Some graduates go on to perform the thrilling trapeze and tumbling acts of the Cirque du Soleil (Circus of the Sun), a world-famous group based in Montréal.

Montréal's well-known annual film festival features the latest movies from around the world. A jazz festival held every July has people dancing in the

Each summer, the community of Drummondville, Québec, hosts the World Folklore Festival.

Small county fairs throughout Québec feature livestock exhibits and parades, as well as rides, foods, and prizes.

streets. Québec City hosts a 10-day winter carnival, the largest such event in the world. The popular carnival includes parades, a snow-sculpture contest, and a boat race across the partly frozen St. Lawrence River.

Winter lasts a long time in Québec. Some people try to avoid it by heading for Montréal's Underground City. More than 29 kilometres (18 miles) of tunnels lined with stores and restaurants link office buildings, hotels, and theatres. People who live in downtown apartment buildings can take the subway to work, go to an underground bank on the way home, and never go outside.

Montréal Canadiens

Many Quebecers are big sports fans, especially when it comes to hockey. The province's National Hockey League team, the Montréal Canadiens, has won the Stanley Cup 24 times. Montréal's baseball team, the Expos, plays ball at the "Big O," as the Olympic Stadium is often called.

Québec has plenty of natural trails for mountain biking (opposite page). ***In spring many Quebecers visit sugar shacks*** (right), ***sometimes riding on horse-drawn wagons!***

Most Quebecers live in towns and cities but love to visit the countryside. In fall, families may go apple picking or drive through the countryside to see the red, gold, and yellow autumn leaves. To greet the spring, many Quebecers visit a *cabane à sucre* (sugar shack) in the country. After a huge meal of eggs, pancakes, sausages, and baked beans—all smothered in maple syrup—young and old dance in a large hall. Another treat is fresh maple syrup poured onto the snow so it hardens into taffy.

Québec is like a French-speaking island in the sea of mostly English-speaking North America. French Quebecers keep their language and culture strong. They hope it will stay that way for many generations to come.

Famous Quebecers

1 Myriam Bédard (born 1969) is an athlete from Loretteville, a suburb of Québec City. In the 1994 Winter Olympics, she won two gold medals in the biathlon, a sport that combines cross-country skiing and rifle shooting.

2 Lucien Bouchard (born 1938), a politician from Jonquière, Québec, has served as Canada's ambassador to France and as Canada's minister of the environment. In 1996, three months after Québec's Sovereignty Separation Referendum failed, he was elected Quebec's premier.

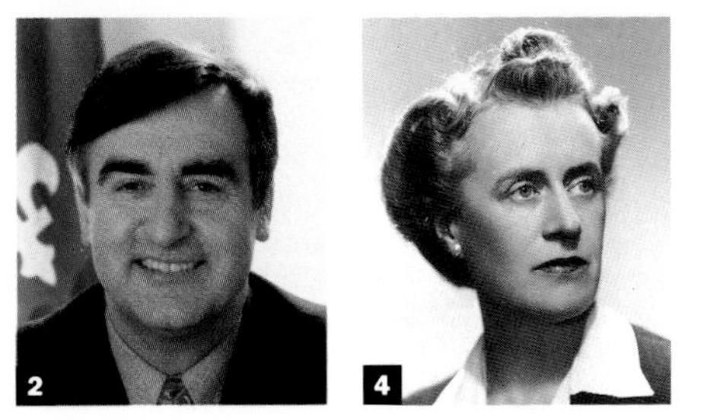

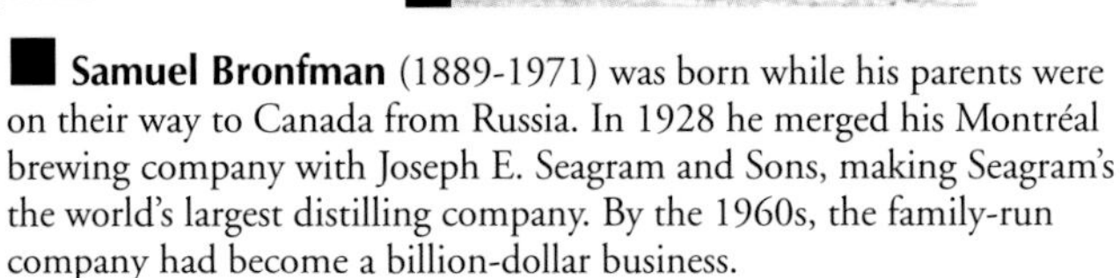

Samuel Bronfman (1889-1971) was born while his parents were on their way to Canada from Russia. In 1928 he merged his Montréal brewing company with Joseph E. Seagram and Sons, making Seagram's the world's largest distilling company. By the 1960s, the family-run company had become a billion-dollar business.

4 Thérèse Casgrain (1896-1981) was a Montréal reformer who worked to win women's right to vote in Québec. In the 1960s, Casgrain helped found the League for Human Rights and the Women's Federation of Québec. In the 1970s, she went on to serve in the Senate.

5 Jean Chrétien (born 1934) is Canada's 20th prime minister. Born in Shawinigan, Québec, he served 23 years in Canada's House of Commons. Elected prime minister in 1993, Chrétien has spent much of his ministership embroiled in Québec's sovereignty issue.

6 Leonard Cohen (born 1934) is one of Canada's most influential poets and songwriters. His albums include *The Songs of Leonard Cohen* and *The Future*. In 1993 the Montréal native was elected to the Juno Awards Hall of Fame.

Matthew Coon Come (born 1956), the grand chief of the Cree of Québec, was born near Lake Mistassini. In 1994 he won the Goldman Environmental Prize for his efforts to stop Hydro-Québec from damming the Great Whale River and flooding Cree trapping and hunting grounds. Coon Come is also a leader among Aboriginals opposed to Québec independence.

8 Céline Dion (born 1968) is a popular singer from Charlemagne, Québec. Dion recorded only in French until 1990. Since then, she has released several albums in English, becoming a star in both languages. She has sold more than 125 million albums and in 2001 she was named the world's best selling female artist.

Reginald Fessenden (1866-1932) was an inventor from Milton-Est, Canada East. In 1906 he achieved the world's first two-way voice transmission by radio and made the first public radio broadcast of music and voice on Christmas Eve.

10 Anne Hébert (1916-2000) published her first collection of poems in 1942 but is best known for her novel *Kamouraska,* which was made into a move in 1973. From Ste-Catherine-de-Fossambault, Québec, Hébert won the Governor General's Award in 1975.

Claude Jutra (1930-1986) began his career directing movies for Canada's National Film Board in the 1950s. He is best known for *Mon oncle Antoine,* one of the most popular films ever made in Canada. Jutra was from Montréal.

12 Kate (born 1946) and **Anna** born (1944) **McGarrigle** are a singing and songwriting folk duo from Montréal. The sisters' albums include *Kate and Anna McGarrigle, Dancer with Bruised Knee* and *The McGarrigle Hour.* They record in both English and French.

■ **John Molson** (1763-1836) came to Montréal from England in 1782. With his sons, he established what is now Molson Companies, Ltd. Besides beer, the billion-dollar company—which is still run by the Molson family—sells lumber and other building materials as well as cleaning products.

14 **Brian Mulroney** (born 1939) was elected to the House of Commons in 1983 and served as Canada's prime minister from 1984 until 1993. Mulroney is from Baie-Comeau, Québec.

■ **Alanis Obomsawin** (born 1932) was raised on the Odanak Reserve, Québec and in Trois-Rivières. An Abenaki singer and filmmaker, she has directed several documentaries, including *Mother of Many Children* and *Incident at Restigouche.* She won a Governor General's Award in 2001.

16 **Oscar Peterson** (born 1925) is an internationally known jazz pianist from Montréal. He has won several Grammy and Juno Awards. In 1973 Peterson was elected to the Order of Canada, and he became a member of the Juno Awards Hall of Fame in 1982.

■ **Maurice ("Rocket") Richard** (1921-2000) played hockey for the Montréal Canadiens from 1942 until 1960. Known as the greatest scorer on his time, he led the National Hockey League in goals scored five times and won the Hart Trophy in 1947. Richard was born in Montréal.

18 **Mordecai Richler** (1931-2000) is an award-winning author from Montréal. *The Apprenticeship of Duddy Kravitz* and *Joshua Then and Now* are among his many novels. Richler has also written books for children, including *Jacobb Two-Two and the Dinosaur.* He last novel, *Barney's Version,* won the Giller Prize in 1998.

■ **Jean-Paul Riopelle** (born 1923) is an abstract artist from Montréal. He has experimented with many techniques, including squeezing paint directly onto the canvas. In 1962 he received the UNESCO Award for his work.

20 **Gabrielle Roy** (1909-1983) lived in Montréal for many years before settling in Québec City. She is well known for her novel *Bonheur d'occasion (The Tin Flute)* and has written stories for children. Roy won the Governor General's Award in 1947, 1957, and 1977.

21 **Bruny Surin** (born 1967) was born in Haiti but has lived in Montréal since he was seven years old. One of the world's top sprinters, Surin was named the International Amateur Athletic Federation's outstanding male athlete in 1993, and won an Olympic gold medal in 1996.

22 **C. J. (Carrie) Taylor** (born 1952), from Montréal, became interested in Aboriginal legends when she learned of her own Mohawk ancestry as a young girl. She writes and illustrates Aboriginal legends for children. Among her titles is *How Two-Feather Was Saved from Loneliness.*

23 **Pierre Trudeau** (1919-2000), a politician from Montréal, served as Canada's prime minister from 1968 until 1979 and again from 1980 until 1984. As prime minister, Trudeau helped make French and English the official languages of Canada. He also worked to add the Canadian Charter of Rights and Freedoms to the Canadian Constitution in 1982.

■ **Manon Vennat** (born 1942) was raised in Montréal. A lawyer, she founded the Business Linguistic Centre in 1972 to help businesses interpret Canada's language laws. In 1986 she was elected the first female and the first Francophone president of the Montréal Board of Trade.

Fast Facts

Provincial Symbols

Motto: *Je me souviens* (I remember)
Nickname: *La Belle Province* (The Beautiful Province)
Flower: iris versicolore
Tree: bouleau jaune
Bird: Snowy owl
Tartan: blue for the upper division of the provincial coat of arms containing three *fleurs de lys,* red for the centre division, gold for the lion in the same division and the crown on the crest, green for the sprig of maple leaves on the lower division, and white for the scroll bearing the provincial motto.

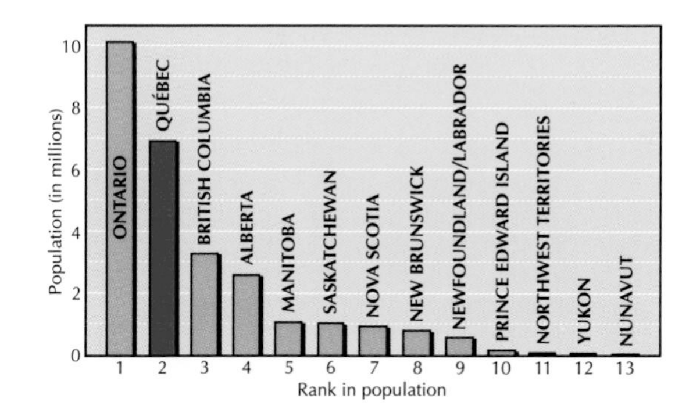

Provincial Highlights

Landmarks: Canadian Museum of Civilization in Hull, Old Montréal and Old Québec, the Citadel in Québec City, Manic-Outardes Complex near Baie-Comeau, Les Forges du Saint-Maurice National Historic Park near Trois-Rivières, Magdalen Islands in the Gulf of St. Lawrence, Village Québécois d'Antan in Drummondville

Annual events: Maple festivals in the Eastern Townships (March), International Fireworks Festival in Montréal (May/June), Canadian Grand Prix in Montréal (June), Shrimp Festival in Matane (June/July), Québec Summer Festival in Québec City (July), Just for Laughs Festival in Montréal (July), Hot-Air Balloon Festival in Gatineau (Sept.), Snow Goose Festival in Montmagny (Oct.)

Professional sports teams: Montréal Expos (baseball); Montréal Canadiens (hockey)

Population*: 7,345,390
Rank in population, nationwide: 2nd
Population distribution: 78 percent urban; 22 percent rural
Population density: 5.3 people per sq km (13.7 per sq mi)
Capital: Québec (671,889 metro area)
Major cities (and populations*): Montréal (3,326,510 metro area), Sherbrooke (76,786), Chicoutimi (63,061), Hull (62,339), Trois-Rivières (48,419)
Major ethnic groups*: French, 75 percent; Aboriginal peoples, 7 percent; British Isles, 4 percent; Italian, 3 percent; German, Polish, Ukrainian, and Dutch, 1 percent total; other backgrounds, 16 percent

***1996 census;** Québec government Website

Endangered Species

Birds: piping plover, reseate tern
Mammals: beluga whale, wolverine

Geographic Highlights

Area (land/water): 1,540,680 sq km (594,857 sq mi)
Rank in area, nationwide: 2nd
Highest Point: Mount D'lberville (1,622m/ 5,322 ft)
Major lakes: Mistassini, Manicouagan Reservoir, Gouin Reservoir, L'Eau-Claire, Bienville, Saint-Jean
Major rivers: St. Lawrence, Eastmain, Great Whale, George, aux Feuilles, Ottawa, Saguenay, St. Maurice, Manicouagan

Economy

Percentage of Workers Per Job Sector

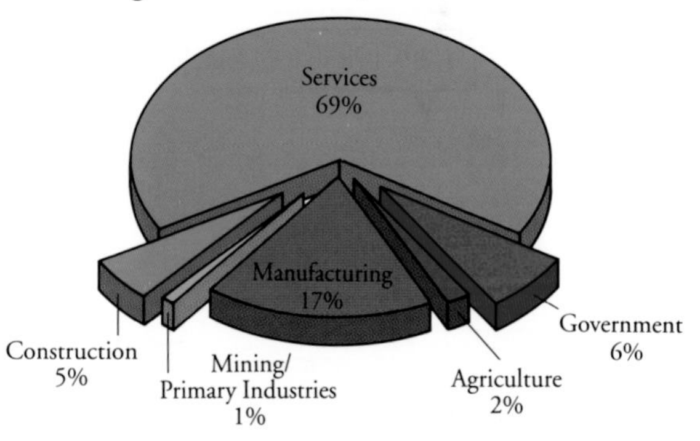

Natural resources: iron ore, copper, lead, zinc, asbestos, nickel, gold, graphite, magnesite, molybdenum, silica
Agricultural products: dairy and beef cattle, hogs, chickens, sheep, turkeys, potatoes, lettuce, peas, tomatoes, apples, blueberries, corn, barley, oats, tobacco, wheat, maple products
Manufactured goods: dairy products, meats, beer, candy, canned fruits and vegetables, coffee, tea, livestock feed, newsprint, paper products, aluminum, steel, pharmaceuticals, industrial chemicals, toiletries, aircraft, automobiles, trains, buses, clothing, telecommunications equipment

Energy

Electric power: hydroelectric (95 percent), nuclear power (5 percent)

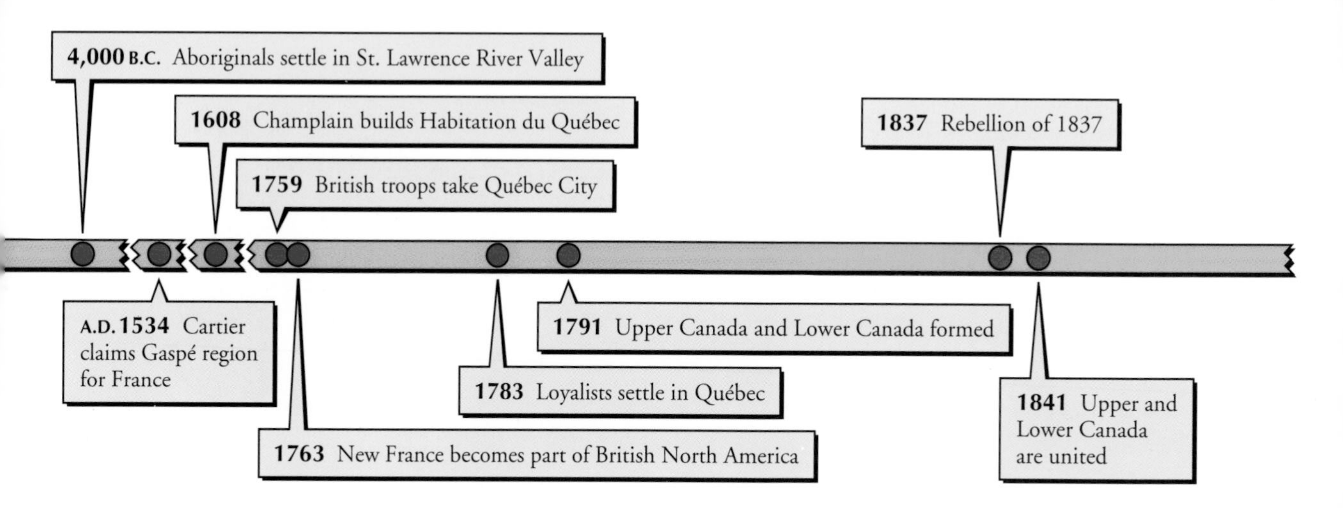

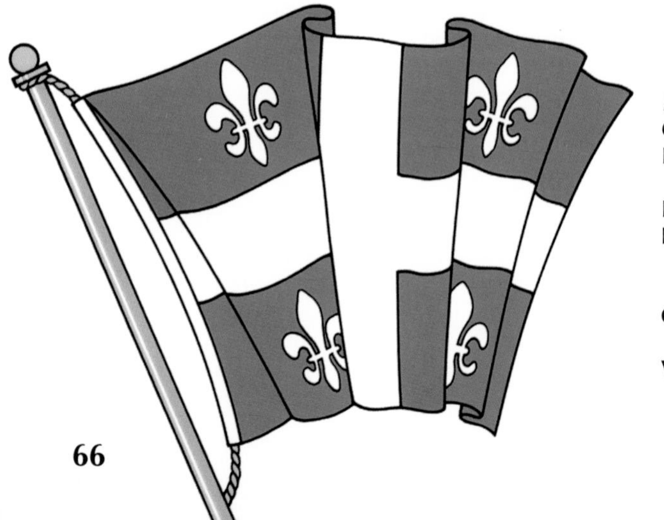

Federal Government

Capital: Ottawa

Head of state: British Crown, represented by the governor general

Head of government: prime minister

Parliament: Senate–105 members appointed by the governor general; House of Commons–301 members elected by the people

Québec representation in parliament: 24 senators; 75 house members

Voting age: 18

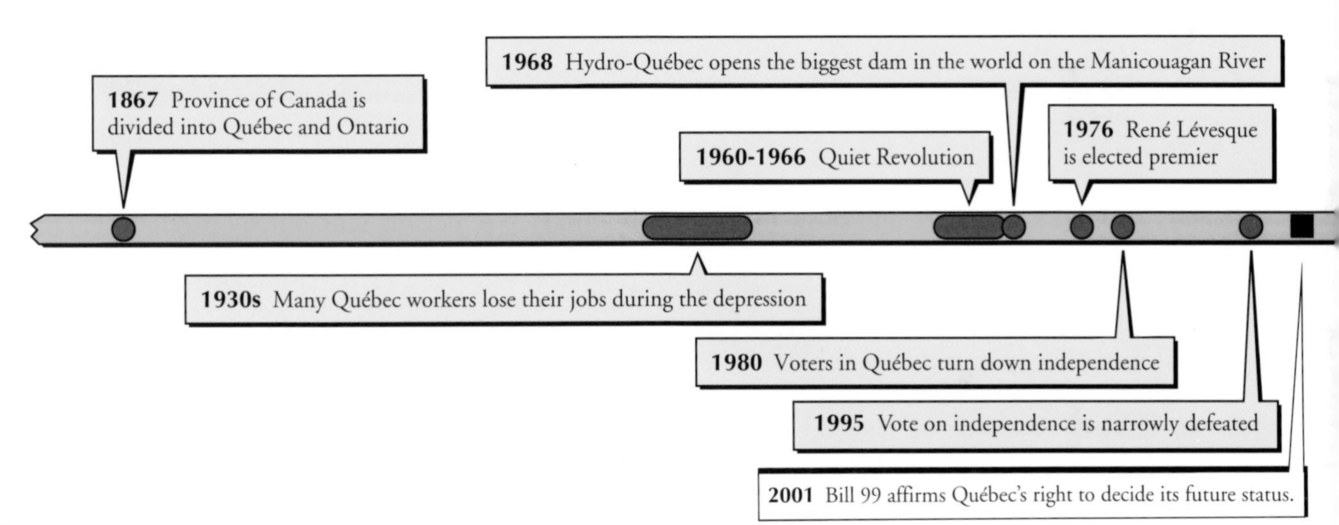

Provincial Government

Capital: Québec
Crown representative: British Crown, represented by the lieutenant governor
Head of government: premier
Cabinet: ministers appointed by the premier
National Assembly: 125 members elected to terms that can last up to 5 years
Voting age: 18 years
Major political parties: Liberal, Parti Québécois

Government Services

To help pay the people who work for Québec's government, the people of Québec pay taxes on money they earn and on many of the items they buy. The services run by the provincial government help assure the people of Québec of a high quality of life. Government funds pay for medical care, for education, for road building and repairs, and for other facilities such as libraries and parks. In addition, the government has funds to help people who are disabled, elderly, or poor.

Glossary

glacier A large body of ice and snow that flows down mountain valleys, often following paths originally formed by rivers. The term is also used to refer to masses of ice that move slowly over the land's surface.

Great Lakes A chain of five lakes in Canada and the northern United States. They are Lakes Superior, Michigan, Huron, Erie, and Ontario.

hydroelectricity The electricity produced by using waterpower. This source of energy is also called hydropower.

loyalist A person who supports the government during a revolt. The term *Loyalist* refers to people who supported Great Britain during the American Revolution (1775–1783).

missionary A person sent out by a religious group to spread its beliefs to other people.

precipitation Rain, snow, and other forms of moisture that fall to earth.

referendum A special election in which voters decide whether to pass a proposed measure into law.

reserve Public land set aside by the government to be used by Aboriginal peoples.

tundra A treeless plain found in arctic and subarctic regions. The ground beneath the top layer of soil is permanently frozen, but the topsoil thaws for a short period each summer, allowing mosses, lichens, and dwarf shrubs to grow.

Pronunciation Guide

Abenaki (a-buh-NAH-kee)

Algonquian (al-GAHN-kwee-uhn)

Appalachian (ap-uh-LAY-chuhn)

Bombardier, Joseph-Armand
(boh^n-bahr-DYAY, zhoh-ZEHF-ahr-MAW^n)

Cartier, Jacques
(kahr-TYAY, ZHAHK)

Champlain, Samuel de
(shaw^n-PLA^n, sah-mew-EHL duh)

Chicoutimi (shuh-KOO-tuh-mee)

Gaspé (ga-SPAY)

Inuit (EE-noo-eet)

Iroquois (IHR-uh-kwoy)

Laurentian, or Laurentides
(law-REHN(t)-shuhn, law-raw^n-TEED)

Lévesque, René (lay-VEHK, ruh-NAY)

Manicouagan (man-uh-KWAHG-uhn)

Métis (may-TEE)

Micmac (MIHK-mak)

Montréal
(moh^n-ray-AHL, muhn-tree-AWL)

Parizeau, Jacques
(pah-ree-ZOH, ZHAHK)

Parti Patriote
(pahr-TEE pah-tree-OHT)

Parti Québécois
(pahr-TEE kay-bay-KWAH)

Québec (kay-BEHK, kwih-BEHK)

Rouyn (roo-WA^n, ROO-uhn)

Saguenay (sag-uh-NAY)

Shawinigan (shuh-WIHN-ih-guhn)

Trois-Rivières (trwah-ree-VYEHR)

Index

About the Author

Janice Hamilton is a writer and freelance journalist who worked for several years in the Montréal bureau of The Canadian Press. As a freelancer, she covers a wide range of issues, from the environment to immigration laws. Her articles have appeared in a variety of publications, including the *Canadian Medical Association Journal* and *Canadian Geographic.* Ms. Hamilton lives in Montréal with her husband and two sons. This is her first book written for children.

Acknowledgments

Laura Westlund, pp. 1, 3, 64, 65 (top), 66-67; Benoît Chalifour, pp. 2, 7, 9,15, 16 (both), 18, 19, 24, 40, 46 (left), 47, 50, 51 (both), 55, 56, 57, 59, 71; Terry Boles, pp. 6, 12, 44, 65 (bottom); Voscar, The Maine Photographer, pp. 8, 42, 49 (left); Jerry Hennen, pp. 10, 11 (top), 21 (top & centre); Alain Dumas, pp. 11 (bottom), 17, 20, 28, 49 (right), 54, 58 (right); Mapping Specialists Ltd., pp. 12–13, 43; © Rob Simpson, p. 21 (bottom left); National Museum of the American Indian/Smithsonian Institution, neg. no.14656, p. 23 (top); Peabody Essex Museum, Salem, MA, p. 23 (bottom); Peabody Museum, Harvard University, Photo by Hillel Burger, p. 25; Confederation Life Gallery of Canadian History, pp. 26, 31, 35; National Archives of Canada, pp. 27 (C1026), 33 (C393), 36 (C2643), 38 (C9338), 60 (centre right/C68509); Historic Urban Plans, Ithaca, N.Y., p. 30; UPI/Bettmann, p. 44; © Robert Fried, pp. 45, 46 (right), 48 (both), 52; © Piotrek B. Gorski, p. 53 (left); Maggi Moetell, p. 53 (right); A. Pichette/CHC, p. 58 (left); Office of the Leader of the Opposition, p. 60 (centre left); Office of the Prime Minister, p. 60 (bottom left); Scott Newton/Austin City Limits, p. 60 (bottom right); Monic Richard, p. 61 (top); Archives nationales du Québec, pp. 61 (centre, Québec-Presse Collection), 62 (centre, Armour Landing Collection), 63 (bottom, Québec-Presse Collection); William Múrphy, p. 61 (bottom); Reuters/Bettmann, p. 62 (top); Erwin, Schenkelbach, p. 62 (bottom); La Société historique de Saint-Boniface, p. 63 (top left); Canadian Sport Images, photo by C. Andersen, p. 63 (top right); Norman Keene, p. 63 (centre).